Let's Dance

African Dancing

By Mark Thomas

Children's Press
A Division of Grolier Publishing
New York / London / Hong Kong / Sydney
Danbury, Connecticut

Photo Credits: Cover and all photos by Maura Boruchow
Contributing Editor: Jeri Cipriano
Book Design: Christopher Logan

Visit Children's Press on the Internet at:
http://publishing.grolier.com

Library of Congress Cataloging-in-Publication Data

Thomas, Mark, 1963-
   African dancing / Mark Thomas.
     p. cm. — (Let's dance)
   Includes bibliographical references and index.
   ISBN 0-516-23141-3 (lib. bdg.)—ISBN 0-516-23066-2 (pbk.)
   1. Dance—Africa—Juvenile literature. 2. Dance, Black—Juvenile literature. [1.
Dance—Africa. 2. Dance, Black.] I. Title.

GV1705 .T56 2000
793.3'196—dc21

00-043187

Contents

My name is Tamika.

I am learning African dance.

African dancing is done **barefoot.**

We don't wear shoes when we dance.

African dancing is danced to African music.

African music uses **drums.**

We watch our teacher dance to the **drumbeat.**

We follow her **dance steps** to learn how to dance.

Sometimes we **slide** our feet.

Sometimes we **stomp** our feet.

We move our arms and bodies, too.

We are dancing in a show.

We wear African **costumes** for the show.

The dances tell stories.

The stories are about African life.

Some dance moves tell about sad things.

Other dance moves tell about happy things.

The drumbeat helps us dance.

The lights show off our costumes.

We like dancing for a **crowd.**

New Words

barefoot (**bair**-foot) not wearing shoes

costumes (**cos**-toomz) clothes worn for a
   show or a party

crowd (**kroud**) many people

dance steps (**dans stepz**) ways to move
   your feet while dancing

drumbeat (**drum**-beet) the sound drums
   make when hit over and over

drums (**drumz**) musical instruments that
   make sounds when hit

slide (**slyd**) to move smoothly

stomp (**stomp**) to bring down your feet
   with force

To Find Out More

Books

Dance

by Angela Shelf Medearis and Michael R. Medearis

Henry Holt & Company

Mimi's Tutu

by Tynia Thomassie

Scholastic

Web Site

AFRO-Americ@: Kids Zone

http://www.afroam.org/children/children.html

This site contains information about Africa. You can play games and read fun facts. It also includes stories that teach about Africa.

Index

About the Author

Mark Thomas is a writer and educator who lives in Florida.